SCIENCE KIDS

Natural or Man-Made

Aaron Carr

LET'S READ AV² BY WEIGL™
ADDED VALUE • AUDIO VISUAL

Go to **www.av2books.com**, and enter this book's unique code.

BOOK CODE

F350772

AV² by Weigl brings you media enhanced books that support active learning.

AV² provides enriched content that supplements and complements this book. Weigl's AV² books strive to create inspired learning and engage young minds in a total learning experience.

Your AV² Media Enhanced books come alive with...

Audio
Listen to sections of the book read aloud.

Video
Watch informative video clips.

Embedded Weblinks
Gain additional information for research.

Try This!
Complete activities and hands-on experiments.

Key Words
Study vocabulary, and complete a matching word activity.

Quizzes
Test your knowledge.

Slide Show
View images and captions, and prepare a presentation.

... and much, much more!

Published by AV² by Weigl
350 5th Avenue, 59th Floor
New York, NY 10118
Website: www.av2books.com   www.weigl.com

Library of Congress Control Number: 2012941987
ISBN 978-1-61913-087-6 (hardcover)
ISBN 978-2-62924-757-8 (softcover)

Printed in the United States of America in North Mankato, Minnesota
3 4 5 6 7 8 9 18 17 16 15 14

062014
WEP040614

Project Coordinator: Aaron Carr   Design: Mandy Christiansen

Weigl acknowledges Getty Images, iStock, and Dreamstime as image suppliers for this title.

Natural or Man-Made

CONTENTS

Some things are natural. These things can be found in nature.

4

Other things are man-made. These things are made by people.

Oranges are natural.

Orange juice is man-made.

6

Orange juice is made from oranges.

Wheat is natural.

Bread is man-made.

Bread is made from wheat.

Corn is natural.

Fuel is man-made.

Some fuels are made from corn.

Trees are natural.

Lumber is man-made.

12

Lumber is made from trees.

Clay is natural.

Bricks are man-made.

14

Bricks are made from clay.

Rubber trees are natural.

Rubber is man-made.

Rubber is made from rubber trees.

Sheep fur is natural.

Wool is man-made.

Wool is made from sheep fur.

Cotton plants are natural.

Cotton is man-made.

Cotton is made from cotton plants.

Which things are natural?
Which things are man-made?

22

23

KEY WORDS

Research has shown that as much as 65 percent of all written material published in English is made up of 300 words. These 300 words cannot be taught using pictures or learned by sounding them out. They must be recognized by sight. This book contains 14 common sight words to help young readers improve their reading fluency and comprehension. This book also teaches young readers several important content words, such as proper nouns. These words are paired with pictures to aid in learning and improve understanding.

Sight Words

are	is
be	made
by	other
can	people
found	some
from	these
in	things

Content Words

bread	lumber	rubber trees
bricks	man-made	sheep fur
clay	natural	trees
corn	nature	wheat
cotton	orange juice	wool
cotton plants	oranges	
fuel	rubber	

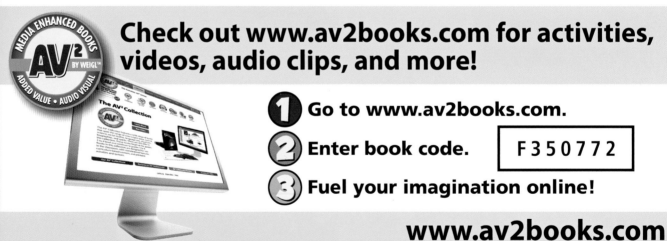

MEDIA ENHANCED BOOKS
AV² BY WEIGL™
ADDED VALUE • AUDIO VISUAL

Check out www.av2books.com for activities, videos, audio clips, and more!

The AV² Collection

1 Go to www.av2books.com.

2 Enter book code.   F 3 5 0 7 7 2

3 Fuel your imagination online!

www.av2books.com

INCREDIBLE ANIMAL LIFE CYCLES
LIFE CYCLE OF A
SNAKE

by Karen Latchana Kenney

pogo

Ideas for Parents and Teachers

Pogo Books let children practice reading informational text while introducing them to nonfiction features such as headings, labels, sidebars, maps, and diagrams, as well as a table of contents, glossary, and index.

Carefully leveled text with a strong photo match offers early fluent readers the support they need to succeed.

Before Reading

- "Walk" through the book and point out the various nonfiction features. Ask the student what purpose each feature serves.
- Look at the glossary together. Read and discuss the words.

Read the Book

- Have the child read the book independently.
- Invite him or her to list questions that arise from reading.

After Reading

- Discuss the child's questions. Talk about how he or she might find answers to those questions.
- Prompt the child to think more. Ask: Have you ever seen snake eggs? What more would you like to learn about snakes after reading this book?

Pogo Books are published by Jump!
5357 Penn Avenue South
Minneapolis, MN 55419
www.jumplibrary.com

Library of Congress Cataloging-in-Publication Data

Names: Kenney, Karen Latchana, author.
Title: Life cycle of a snake / by Karen Latchana Kenney.
Description: Minneapolis, MN : Jump!, Inc., [2018]
Series: Incredible animal life cycles
"Pogo Books are published by Jump!" | Includes index.
Identifiers: LCCN 2017060205 (print)
LCCN 2017059761 (ebook)
ISBN 9781624968235 (ebook)
ISBN 9781624968211 (hardcover : alk. paper)
ISBN 9781624968228 (pbk.)
Subjects: LCSH: Snakes–Life cycles–Juvenile literature.
Classification: LCC QL666.O6 (print)
LCC QL666.O6 K46 2018 (ebook) | DDC 597.96156–dc23
LC record available at https://lccn.loc.gov/2017060205

Editor: Jenna Trnka
Book Designer: Molly Ballanger

Photo Credits: Eric Isselee/Shutterstock, cover (top), cover (bottom), 1, 3, 23; Ingo Arndt/Minden Pictures, 4; Heiko Kiera/Shutterstock, 5; blickwinkel/Alamy, 6-7; E R DEGGINGER/Getty, 8-9; Biosphoto/SuperStock, 10; Rick &Nora Bowers/Alamy, 11; Butterfly Hunter/Shutterstock, 12-13; Nick Garbutt/Minden Pictures, 14-15; Kurit afshen/Shutterstock, 16; Mark Kostich/iStock, 17; FLPA/Alamy, 18-19; M. Watsonantheo/Pantheon/SuperStock, 20-21.

Printed in the United States of America at Corporate Graphics in North Mankato, Minnesota.

TABLE OF CONTENTS

CHAPTER 1

....

TEARING FREE

Rip, rip. A small, soft snake egg rips open. Out pokes a tiny head. A sharp **egg tooth** helps the **snakelet** tear free.

egg tooth

The snakelet slowly slithers out. It uncurls its long body for the first time. This is just one step in the snake's incredible life cycle.

Most snakes **hatch** from eggs. The mother finds a warm, dark, and damp spot. She then lays her eggs on the ground or in a nest. She leaves her **clutch** of eggs. They will hatch on their own.

But other snakes stay to protect their eggs. Some warm their eggs, too. Pythons curl around their eggs. They **brood** until the eggs hatch.

python

snakelet

There are around 3,000 different kinds of snakes. Most of these **reptiles** lay eggs. But some give birth to live snakelets. The **embryos** grow in eggs. But the eggs hatch inside the mother. Then the snakelets emerge.

CHAPTER 2

HUNTING

A snakelet can take care of itself right away. It flicks out its forked tongue. Why? It uses its tongue to smell the air. This hungry baby is searching for food.

It slithers across the ground. What does it smell? Baby mice or frog eggs. Insects and earthworms make good meals, too. Snakes are **carnivores**. This growing snakelet needs to eat so it can grow.

Snakes become expert hunters. But not all snakes hunt the same way. For example, vipers and cobras have **venom**. It comes out of their sharp fangs. The fangs sink into **prey**. The venom shoots into the animal. It paralyzes the meal.

DID YOU KNOW?

Snake teeth are not designed to chew. So snakes swallow their prey whole. Their jaws can open wider than their bodies!

But boas and other snakes don't have venom. They strike prey with their fangs. Then they wrap their big, strong bodies around the animal. They **constrict** to kill. Then they swallow their meal.

DID YOU KNOW?

Green anacondas are some of the world's biggest snakes. They constrict their prey, which can also be very large. These snakes can swallow cows whole!

CHAPTER 3
SHEDDING AND MATING

Scales cover a snake's body like armor. They protect the baby snake. But to grow, the snake has to shed a layer of its skin.

skin

It rubs its head on a rock. This splits the skin. The snake rolls its old skin off in one long piece. As a snake sheds, it grows. In a few years, it will be an adult.

Adult snakes in different areas **mate** at different times. Snakes are **cold-blooded**. They depend on sunlight and warm temperatures to keep warm. Because of this, snakes in colder areas mate in early spring so that snakelets are born in warmer months.

Snakes that live in tropical areas can mate year-round. Why? Because it is always warm.

TAKE A LOOK!

Each snake goes through a life cycle. It has three **stages**:

egg:
An embryo grows for a few months or more in its egg.

adult:
An adult snake never stops growing.

snakelet:
A snakelet grows for two to five years to become an adult.

female

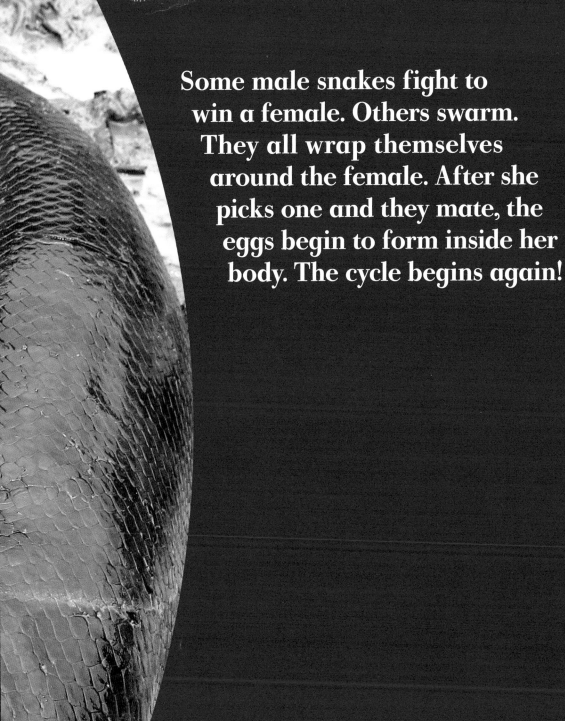

Some male snakes fight to win a female. Others swarm. They all wrap themselves around the female. After she picks one and they mate, the eggs begin to form inside her body. The cycle begins again!

ACTIVITIES & TOOLS

SHEDDING SKIN

Look at a snake's shed skin. You can see patterns. They show the snake's scales. Try this activity to shed some skin. What will you see?

What You Need:
- white glue
- your hand

1. **Spread a thin layer of white glue on the palm of your hand. This is like a layer of skin.**

2. **Let it dry. Don't touch anything!**

3. **Now carefully peel off the layer of glue. Try to keep it all in one piece like a snakeskin.**

4. **Wash your hands well with soap.**

5. **Now look at the glue you peeled off. What patterns do you see? You should see lines from your hand. It has your hand's pattern, just like a snake's skin keeps its pattern.**

GLOSSARY

brood: To sit on eggs to make them hatch.

carnivores: Animals that eat other animals as food.

clutch: A group of eggs laid together.

cold-blooded: Having a body temperature that changes according to the surrounding temperature.

constrict: To squeeze tightly.

egg tooth: The small, sharp tooth on a snakelet's upper lip that is used to tear open the egg.

embryos: Animals in the earliest stage of their life cycle.

hatch: To break out of an egg.

mate: When a male and female animal come together to make babies.

prey: An animal that is hunted by another animal for food.

reptiles: Cold-blooded animals that crawl or move on their bellies or on short, small legs.

snakelet: A newborn snake.

stages: Steps or periods of development.

venom: A poison a snake injects into its prey.

INDEX

TO LEARN MORE

Learning more is as easy as 1, 2, 3.

1) Go to www.factsurfer.com

2) Enter "lifecycleofasnake" into the search box.

3) Click the "Surf" button to see a list of websites.

With factsurfer, finding more information is just a click away.

For A.M.B.
H.Z.

For Prosper
C.S.

VIKING KESTREL
Published by the Penguin Group
Viking Penguin Inc., 40 West 23rd Street, New York, New York 10010, U.S.A.
Penguin Books Ltd, 27 Wrights Lane, London W8 5TZ England
Penguin Books Australia Ltd, Ringwood, Victoria, Australia
Penguin Books Canada Ltd, 2801 John Street, Markham, Ontario, Canada L3R 1B4
Penguin Books (N.Z.) Ltd, 182–190 Wairau Road, Auckland 10, New Zealand

Penguin Books Ltd, Registered Offices: Harmondsworth, Middlesex, England

First published in 1988 by Viking Penguin Inc.

Published simultaneously in Canada

Text copyright © Harriet Ziefert, 1988

Illustrations copyright © Claire Schumacher, 1988

All rights reserved
ISBN 0-670-82423-2
Library of Congress catalog card number: 88-80668

Printed in Singapore for Harriet Ziefert, Inc.
Set in

1 2 3 4 5 92 91 90 89 88

Harriet Ziefert

Illustrated by Claire Schumacher

Viking Kestrel

The snow had been falling quietly
all night long.

By morning a thick blanket of white covered
the countryside. It seemed as if nothing
existed in the world but beautiful snow.

Suddenly, as if by magic, snow women, and
snow men, and snow children began to appear.
Some carried boxes; some carried bags.

"Here is a perfect spot!" said a snow woman.
"Yes!" said a snow man. "Let's put everything
down right here."

All of the snow people began to work.
While one hammered a post into the ground,
two others opened a table.

"What's in this big box?" a snow boy asked.
"You'll see soon," said his mother.

"Sweeping the pond is hard," said a child. "Right," said his friend. "But tonight is going to be great. We've found a special place for a special party."

The musicians arrived in the late afternoon.

Everything was almost ready.

Now the party could begin.

"Come one. Come all. Come gather around!" called a man. "Today we celebrate the first day of winter. When the first snow of the year falls on the first day of winter, we can have a snow party!"

Everybody clapped and cheered.
Hooray for winter! Hooray for snow!

And the snow people ate…

and danced…

and sang.

At midnight snow began to fall.
The snow fell and fell—very quietly.

It was still falling as the party-goers
went on their way.

By morning a new blanket of white covered
the countryside. It seemed as if nothing
existed in the world but beautiful snow.

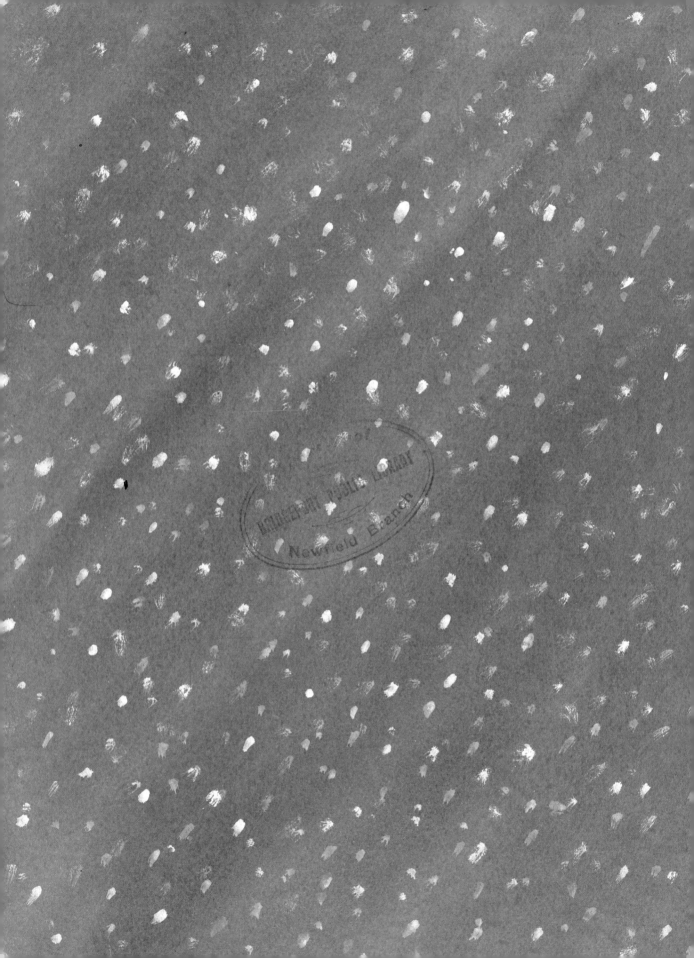